WAKE UP, KIDS

WAKE UP, KIDS

HUBERT SEVERE

XULON PRESS

Xulon Press
2301 Lucien Way #415
Maitland, FL 32751
407.339.4217
www.xulonpress.com

© 2021 by Hubert Severe

All rights reserved solely by the author. The author guarantees all contents are original and do not infringe upon the legal rights of any other person or work. No part of this book may be reproduced in any form without the permission of the author. The views expressed in this book are not necessarily those of the publisher.

Unless otherwise indicated, Scripture quotations taken from the New King James Version (NKJV). Copyright © 1982 by Thomas Nelson, Inc. Used by permission. All rights reserved.

Scripture quotations taken from the English Standard Version (ESV). Copyright © 2001 by Crossway, a publishing ministry of Good News Publishers. Used by permission. All rights reserved.

Scripture quotations taken from the Holy Bible, New International Version (NIV). Copyright © 1973, 1978, 1984, 2011 by Biblica, Inc.™. Used by permission. All rights reserved.

Printed in the United States of America.

Paperback ISBN-13: 978-1-66281-091-6
Ebook ISBN-13: 978-1-66281-092-3

Table of Contents

Preface vii
Introduction: Be an Example to Our Children ix

#1: Show Children the Reality of Life 1
#2: A Parent's Prayer 3
#3: My Life 5
#4: The Power of Love 9
#5: The Reality of Life 11
#6: The Lord Is Real 15
#7: A Note to Parents 19
#8: Love Your Parents 23
#9: Education 27
#10: Money 31
#11: Love and Relationships 35
#12: Fear Is Your Worst Enemy 39
#13: Learn From Our Mistakes 43

#14: Learn to Work Together 47
#15: Secrets 51
#16: Respect Yourself and Others 55
#17: All Lives Matter 59

Conclusion: Promises from God. 61

Preface

A Book for Parents and Children Thirteen-Years-Old and Up

I write this book to share my advice to parents and children thirteen years old and older to help them navigate through life. In fact, this book will benefit parents and children from generation to generation. I just want to make sure that they don't fall in the same hole as I did as a parent and as a child. My life is horrible right now and I don't want you to have the same life I had growing up. I want you to keep in mind that the easy way doesn't mean it is the right way. All you need to do in life is to try your best to do things the right way.

This world belongs to the youth who will be the leaders of tomorrow. We all need to take good care of it by loving, appreciating, respecting it, and supporting one another as we should do.

Parents, we need to tell the youth the truth and set a good example by doing what is right specially to one another. We are the present and need to make sure our next generation have a good world to grow up in. You need to get it cleaned up and make it safe. Right now, we are living in a deteriorating, unsafe environment.

Children, I know that we make mistakes as parents, but you shouldn't make the same mistakes we did. You need to learn from our mistakes. That is what I hope to achieve by writing this book. Do unto others as you will want them to do unto you.

Introduction

BE AN EXAMPLE FOR OUR CHILDREN

My brothers and sisters, I want to share some insights I have learned about the way we treat each other and the way we serve the Lord. We completely need to change because our kids are walking right behind us and going to follow in our footsteps. Let us do things the right way and follow the right direction so they can do the same. We need to teach them the Word of God and explain to them why we call on the Lord's name and what can happen to them when they say it.

Without the love of God, our life wouldn't make any sense. Why don't we want to explain this truth to our kids? Is it because we love them too much that we don't want to hurt them? Or is it because we are too ashamed of the truth? Shame on us. When we will put our families first! We are saying we will, but we don't mean it. If we really meant it, the first thing we would talk to our kids about is the power of praying in the name of the Lord. We would explain to them that our Lord will never leave us and wants only the best for us. Isn't that important enough to tell our kids?

Listen, brothers and sisters, use yourselves as examples. You know the meaning of life and how much you have learned from what you have already done in life, good and bad. You have learned the Lord always forgives you when you repent and ask Him for forgiveness. Don't you think, we should tell our kids the truth so they will not go through the same things we have because of our wrong choices? We are not perfect. But, only if we think before we ask. It will make a big difference. Just think about our kids and that alone can make a big difference in our life. This is my special phrase, shame on us!

We cannot blame anyone else but ourselves if our children make the same mistakes and do not turn to the Lord for guidance as they begin to make choices in their lives. If we really love each other, we need to do what is best for our families. If we have neglected to do that, the Word of God says we are wicked and selfish. This is the reason why we should put our families first. However, the Lord will forgive us, but it is our choice to do things the right way.

Will you make that choice today and show your children how to live a life of blessings from the Lord? This book will help you. Please read it, use it, and pass it on to more parents.

#1:

Show Children the Reality of Life

Dear Parents: We need to begin by showing our kids the reality of life, so our kids can do better for the next generation. Right now, we are calling each other brother and sister, yet we are killing each other in the streets because we are angry and unforgiving. What do we think our kids will do as they get older?

The first example we need to provide for our children is biblical forgiveness. We want God to forgive us, but do we never want to forgive others and even ourselves. Listen, my brothers and sisters. I don't think we will want our kids to go through the same thing that we went through. Right now, we need to sit down and think about what will be best for our kids. Let us try to teach our kids what is right and wrong. Let us pray for these kids every single day for them to have a better life, especially these orphans out there. These kids deserve it. Let us put our knees on the floor and pray for these kids to have a great life. This is not the time to be selfish. We should make sure that we cover the hole we fell into so the next generation will not fall in it. If our parents thought like this, I bet you we could have better peace in this world.

What should parents do for their children, so they don't fall into the same hole we did?

- Prepare your children to live a productive and prosperous life.
- Teach them practical and biblical principles that will give them what they need to bring changes to our world so it will be safe and fruitful for many more generations to come.
- Set a good example of how to do things right.
- Pray for your kids every day. Use the following prayer to get you started.

#2:

A Parent's Prayer

Dear Lord, today I want to thank You for everything You have done for me. I'm very happy to see myself going in this direction because You give me the knowledge to see things differently. God, I want You to forgive me for all the wrong things I have done to other people knowingly and unknowingly and I deeply ask for your forgiveness. My Lord, from now on, I will try my best to do better. I am going to change my life to be better to my fellow brothers and sisters. I want to show my kids the true meaning of being loving to my brothers and sisters, so they can do the same. I am tired of living this way. I know You will do Your part by keeping me and my children safe and guide us in the right direction as we will do our best to get our part done the right way. I know my family deserves a better life.

I know I need to guide them in a better direction so they will do the same for their family. It is time for me to build a better world for my family. Please, Lord, I know nothing is impossible with You. Please take great care of me and my kids as I strive to do what is right. I will do my part and leave the rest in Your hands. I know You will never leave me and I truly believe that You will do the same for my kids. I love You, my Lord. You will always be my guide and protector. Thank you my Lord. Amen!

Parents:

- Post this prayer where you can see it every day.
- Pray it the first thing in the morning as you start your day.
- Pray it the last thing at night before you close your eyes.

#3:

My Life

Dear Children of this generation, I'm writing this letter to explain to you all the things about my life that I hope will help you navigate your life. Right now, I'm living a crazy life. I'm mentally and physically tired. I'm working long hours six days a week. My day off is Saturday. I'm living paycheck to paycheck and I can't even buy a decent amount of food for my family. Most of the time, I have to visit the food pantry because the money I worked for isn't enough to pay my bills.

I am writing this book to share my knowledge so you can achieve a better life than I am living. You always need to start somewhere and work yourself to the place that you want to be.

I'm telling you these things because I don't want this to happen to you. Please, you need to be strong and have faith in the Lord and yourself. You shouldn't let anyone drag you into this kind of life. You need to use the gifts and talents the Lord has given you to move forward and upward in life and be who the Lord wants you to be. You need to be strong in all different ways. Have self-control, especially in your finances. Think before you make your decisions and do what is right before you move forward. You are never too old to ask for help and before you do anything make sure you pray about it first.

This world is yours and no one can take it from you as long as you do things right. You need to stay focused and have faith in the Lord. You need to do your part and let the Lord do His part. You are His children and He will never leave you alone. He wants to make sure that the job gets done the right way. Be patient and let the Lord do His work, His way, and in His timing. That will always be the right way and then you can bring the good news to others.

Please pay a little attention to my stories. I had a friend when I went to English classes in 2001. He was a good friend to me. I respected him and so he respected me. He had a sister who got pregnant and her father kicked her out of his house. She didn't know where to go. She saw me and explained her situation. I helped her to get a place to live and helped her out of all through her pregnancy. I never disrespected her. This is the kind of thing that we need to do for others. We need to help others with our whole heart and never expect anything in return. We all will need each other sometime in our lives.

Don't let evil thoughts control your heart to make you believe that isn't the right thing to do. We all need each other. You always need to share with other people who need it. It doesn't matter who that person is or what they have done to need your help. You need to just give and the Lord will do the rest. When you share and give with your left hand, you will receive with your right hand and never expect that the same person that you helped should help you in return. The Lord is always watching us whether what we do is good or bad. Never do anything halfway. You just need to always try to do your best and to do things the right way. This is what life is about. You need to love everyone even though you know that person doesn't like you. This is the way life works.

My next story is about when I was a kid. I heard others talking about eating all kinds of different foods for breakfast, lunch, and dinner. I didn't know what they were talking about because whatever we had was what we ate. Whatever food I didn't finish one day, I ate the next day for breakfast. There was no choice unless I wanted to stay hungry.

Most of the time, I didn't have soap, shampoo, or skin lotion. Sometimes, I just showered with water, but I did not feel clean. My skin became very dry as we didn't have any lotion either, so I used any type of oil I could find to lubricate my dry skin. Sometimes, it was cooking oil. It made my skin shine, but if there were ants in my classroom, all the oil on my legs would be gone.

Make sure you appreciate what your parents provide for you every day and give thanks to the Lord for His blessings. There were many things that I ate when I was a kid that hopefully, you will never have to eat.

What can we do even though we are still young?

- This world is yours and no one can take it from you as long as you do things right.
- You need to stay focused and have faith in the Lord.
- You need to do your part and let the Lord do His part, His work, His way, and in His timing.
- That will always be the right way and then you can bring the good news to others.

#4:

The Power of Love

L ove is one of the most powerful things in life. Without love, your life can be upside down from a baby until the end of your life. This is the reason you need to understand that the Lord gives us His love and He said the more you share it, the more you will receive. The Lord didn't give you His love to keep it to yourself. He gave you His love to share with everyone. It doesn't matter what you want to do. You have a choice to keep it for yourself, but you will only be truly happy when you share and give it to others. It doesn't matter what they do with it.

One thing I am sure of, though, love is very important for all of us, and without love, we will not thrive in this wonderful world God has given to us. Let us take His love, do something great with it, and leave it for our next generation. Please, do not forget if you don't share it fairly, your share will not be good and blessed by the Lord. You need to be wise in everything you do, including sharing God's love in the right way. He will direct your path if you seek His direction.

Let us use this love as a gift and share it as often as we can with those God sends across our paths. Let us act like real brothers and let us feel like it's raining love everywhere and everyone is soaking with the blessing of love. It's not too difficult. You just need to put your mind to it and let your heart do the rest.

Love Is the Answer:

- Take the love God has given you and do something great with it.
- You need to be wise in everything you do, including sharing God's love in the right way.
- He will direct your path if you seek His direction.
- Use His love as a gift and share it as often as you can with those God sends across your path.

#5:

The Reality of Life

I was born a Roman Catholic and I have been hearing so many bad things about the catholic church. I decided to visit other churches to see the difference for myself. I have learned the difference between catholic church . The catholic churches are giving and helping more than they received. They kept things easy and simple. They teach how the Lord will do His part if we are not greedy. We will have a wonderful world if we share with others as the Lord has directed us. We need to believe in the power of the Lord and praise the Lord every day. We also need to help one another. Children, I'm not telling you to leave your church and go to Catholic Churches, because of material things. I'm telling you this thing to see if you can make a difference in other churches.

Children, there are so many different churches who hate Catholic churches. Please, don't be like these people. Catholic church doesn't talk about other churches. You need to go to whatever church you prefer and follow the rules of the Lord. You need to choose a religion that you like and praise the Lord the right way. You don't need to go to all the different churches to learn the truth like I did. All you need is to read the Bible and use your common sense. You need to go to church and embrace all the good things that could help you and leave all the nonsense behind. You need to set a good example for your next generation. This is the way life works.

Children, the power of the Lord is not magic. But, you can receive his blessings and miracles just like magic. When you really believe in God. He powers and blessings be with you everywhere you go and everything you do. Children do not let anyone to fool you to stop receiving the Glory, miracle and the power of the Lord. You just need to take it and use it. Do not forget to share it with others and use it to save your brothers and sisters life's. For example: spider man and the incredible.

Catholic churches are not perfect, but they tried to make things better by telling the truth. Please children, soon we will leave this planet in your hands. Please, do not take advantage of each other the way we do. In your world, you need to make everyone comfortable in church, not only the rich one who deserves love and appreciation.

The most important thing is the truth. Do not sell or buy the word of God and Do not sell or buy the prayer of the Lord, especially for prayer requests. You need to always give your tithes and offerings. You need to share the words of the Lord and his prayers to one another for free and the Lord will bless you. Only the Lord who can bless us. If you want to buy a private airplane and a goal toilet. Do not take advantage of the people who come in your church to buy them for you and always try to do your best to put your feet in other people's shoes. I always will tell you that, you need to do things the right way children. Right now, we have a million people who stopped going to churches because of that. I don't want you to do the same things we did. But, I want you to do things in a different way or better than us. We are the children of the Lord and the Lord loves us all. It is our choice to love each other and be one nation. Now, we don't care about each other because of our race, color or nations. Children, it doesn't matter where you were born or your color. You are a human just like one another. It is your choice if you do, but you shouldn't say that I didn't tell you.

The Lord is real and He isn't happy with what we are doing to ourselves and to others. Please, children, the world will be yours someday, so do all you can to take care of it in a different and better way. When you take care of what He has given you, the Lord will bless you in all that you do.

You Can Start Today:

- Attend a church that teaches the Bible.
- Learn what the Lord desires of His children.
- Study the life of Jesus in the Bible. Read the books of Matthew, Mark, Luke, and John.
- You will prosper in all that you do when you learn to do what pleases the Lord.

#6:

THE LORD IS REAL

Dear Children, I want to explain to you about the Lord. The Lord is real, though many don't believe it because they can't see Him. Please, pay attention. I just want to tell you what I think is true. I came from Haiti and I know that voodoo is real even though I can't see it. I can see the results and effects it has on those who believe and use it for their own purposes.

Please be smart. The Lord blesses us as we use the gifts and talents He has given us to work and earn everything that we have. It is our choice to believe in Him and His promises to receive His blessings. Satan will offer us his power, but he doesn't give us anything for free. He always wants things in return. The Lord blessed us with things and He never asked for anything in return. Everything that Satan has "given" you is because he needs your soul to do his work. In my country, when you die, the voodoo man asks Satan for permission to take your soul and sell it to other people to make you work for them. They are called zombies.

Listen, when you go to church, don't go because you are bored at home or because you don't have anything else to do. You need to go to church to fight against your enemy. Who is your enemy? Satan! If you are not preparing to do battle with him, when he sends his attacks, you will not have a chance for victory. America will not stop building and training the military not because they are going to war. But, because they always have to be ready, for if in case they have to go to war. They want to be ready for anything. You need to think just like them. It is your life and you have the choice to serve the Lord your way, but you need to serve Him the right way. You can't have one foot in and one foot out. Your two feet need to be in or out. You have to choose.

We need to believe in the Lord, but we need to believe in realities, too. The Lord has given us a choice to select between good and bad, right and wrong. The Lord will not tell us which one to pick. We have our own choices. We have our free will. However, He does warn us of the consequences of our choices. Do not do crazy things because you think that you have God in your life. We are human beings and we make mistakes all the time. The Lord is always going to forgive us, but be careful about the things that you do. There will still be consequences for your actions even though the Lord will forgive you. He will forgive you for not waiting until you are married to have sex, but you will still have to care for the baby you create. It will not disappear because God has forgiven you.

Choose Wisely:

- Please be smart with your choices.
- It is your choice to believe in Him and His promises to receive His blessings.
- The Lord has given you a choice to select between good and bad, right and wrong.
- The Lord will not tell you which one to pick. You have to make your own choices.
- Realize there are consequences to every choice, some good and some bad.

#7:

A Note to Parents

Parents: We are brothers and sisters. We are all part of God's family and are here to care for the world God our Father has given us so it will be here from generation to generation. Life should not be the way it is right now. We are in a big competition. We all want to be better than others. We forget we are a team and should be working together as brothers and sisters.

To be a parent is a big responsibility. Most of the time, you know what is best for your kids. You need to have a good relationship with your immediate family and your extended family. Your brothers and sisters should be your best friends. You need to trust them and be open and free to talk with them about what is going on in your life. Your friend at work shouldn't know your family's secrets because sooner or later they will sell you out.

By the time you grow old, you will probably pass through many types of love, but your family should have the first space in your heart. The first place in your heart should be to love the person who deserves it the most. I'm not telling you to choose that family who treated you poorly over your wonderful spouse or your ridiculous husband's demands over your wonderful family. You just need to be careful when you make your decisions. Sometimes, it takes a lot of thought before you make the right one. Please ask questions and answer the dilemma with your heart and you have a better chance to make the right decision. You always need to love the one who is loving, appreciating, respecting, and supporting you and you need to love everyone even though you know they hate you. Please, do not give anyone fake love. You need to use your real love and share it the right way.

Do not mix love and money together. Money doesn't have anything to do with love and love doesn't have anything to do with money. You can have the world and never have a happy life and sometimes you don't have anything, and you live a happy life.

You are the King and Queen in your family and are the most valuable people not only in your immediate family, but also in your communities and even in your countries. Your parents and grandparents may have put all kinds of nonsense in our minds, but you do not have to teach your kids the same things. The world is very different than before and you need to try to make things different in a good way. Why do you keep using the same traditions? You know some of these traditions are not right. Can you just trust yourself and try to make your own traditions?

Look at all the wonderful new things people are making or building all over the world. Be creative, my brothers and sisters. Let's give our kids a chance to build a better life for themselves. It is okay if you want to walk with them to make sure they are walking in the right direction, but you need to trust them, too.

Let's try to do our best to stay connected with our kids and make them feel they are unique and can achieve great things. Sometimes, because of the choices or traditions from our parents, we have lost our direction, but as a parent, we need to tell our kids the truth and the realities of life. Teach them that anyone who does the right things will achieve in life.

What must we do to be better parents?

To be a parent is a big responsibility. You are the King and Queen in your family and are the most valuable people not only in your immediate family, but also in your communities and even in your countries.

- Try to do your best to stay connected with your kids.
- Make them feel they are unique and can achieve great things.
- Teach them that anyone who does the right things will achieve in life.

#8:

LOVE YOUR PARENTS

We all know there are good parents and bad parents. Most parents have a real love for their kids. However, if you weren't Lucky to have a good parent, learn from their mistakes. You still need to love your parents. They gave you life no matter what the circumstances of your birth. When they get old, please be there for them. Do not stop loving them until the end. If you don't have time to take care of them and then put them in a good care facility and make time at least once a week to visit them. You can bring them anything that you can afford, like flowers or special treats you know they would enjoy.

You need to do the right thing and so you can receive the same blessing from the Lord and from your children when you grow old. You need to make your parents comfortable and treat them right. Don't forget, whatever things you do in life and will follow you to the end. When you do good, good will follow you, but when you do bad, bad will follow you until the end. You can help your parents now and yourself in the future.

If you are a young boy or girl, realize your parents should not be your servants. You need to learn how to help them by helping yourself to learn. All the things that you learn you will use them to become a good husband or wife. There are a number of ways you can learn to take care of yourself. Clean your own room and find ways to help your parents around the house. Helping with the dishes, doing your own laundry, putting groceries away, and cleaning are easy to learn. What you learn can help in the future and for the rest of your life. If you listen to me, you will see how easy your life will be in the future.

Remember: The Bible gives you a command with a promise in Exodus 20:12, "Honor your father and your mother, that your days may be long upon the land which the Lord your God is giving you" (NKJV).

- You need to do the right thing so you can receive the same blessing from the Lord and from your children when you grow old.
- Don't forget, whatever things you do in life and will follow you to the end. When you do good, good will

follow you, but when you do bad, bad will follow you until the end. Choose to do what is good!
- Find ways to help your parents around the house.
- Helping with the dishes, doing your own laundry, putting groceries away, and cleaning are easy to learn.

#9:

Education

There are three things that bring happiness as you grow up in life. A good education, earning enough money to support yourself, and love.

I want to explain why you should strive to achieve a good education. Education is the key which can open every door of opportunity. If you are fortunate enough to have a great parent who is trying to help you and support you to get a good education, please, take advantage of it and appreciate it. If you don't, sooner or later you will regret it. You may have to work hard and find a way to achieve a good education, but you will be glad you did. Everyone has one great chance in life. Now, it's your chance. You need to take it and make sure that you use it.

You may be living a free life at home right now, but soon you will be on your own. The time you have now is for you to prepare for your life when you will be on your own. Please, do not waste your time now. Sooner or later, you will need what you are learning now so you can enjoy yourself and your family in the future. You need to try your best to graduate from high school and earn a college degree. You don't need to be super smart to reach these goals. You just need to use your mind, study, do your part, and the Lord will bless you with the rest. Listen, nothing is impossible in life unless you make it that way. This is your life and you need to think about all the things that you will want in the future.

A good education is one of the best things you can work to achieve in your life. It doesn't matter what anyone says. You need to take school seriously every single day. A good education is the thing that will build your life strong. Don't go to school because you don't have a choice. You need to go to school because that's the right thing to do. You need to think about your future and how you want it to be when you are an adult. If you want to build a strong house, the most important thing is the foundation. The foundation is the thing holding the house together in the storms. You can't have a tree without roots. A good education is the root of your life.

After you graduate from high school, you need to go to college to get a degree. Don't let the fast-food restaurant job destroy your whole life. I understand that you need money for expenses in your life now, but you need to think about a better future. Do you want to do that for the rest of your life? A great future means a good education. Then you need to use what you learn and make use of it. You may know people who graduated from high school and went to college, but never made use of what they learned to build their lives. Please don't be that person. Watch those who go on to use what they have learned to make a good life for themselves and their families and learn from their example.

Education is the key which can open every door of opportunity.

Follow these steps to your great opportunity:

- You need to try your best to graduate from high school and earn a college degree.
- Use your mind, study, do your part, and the Lord will bless you with the rest.
- Nothing is impossible in life unless you make it that way.
- Think about all the things that you will want in the future.
- Build a good foundation starting now.

Remember: A good education is one of the best things you can work to achieve success in your life.

#10:

Money

Many people make money the most important thing in their lives. It is true we need money to pay our bills and provide for our families, but it seems people have made money become the worst evil thing in this world. When we work hard and we get a paycheck, why do we still take advantage of one another in an effort to receive more? Many have let money destroy their relationships and their families. Please, children, the way you are seeing things happening around you doesn't mean it is the way to get ahead in life.

Learn how to spend your money wisely. The money you earn is for you to spend, but you need to spend it in the right way. The COVID-19 crisis should be a good example for us of what can happen. You are working very hard to make your money. You need to spend it for your needs and make sure you save some for emergencies. You should use it for your needs and not everything you want. There is a difference in wants and needs. Meeting your needs should be the priority each time you receive a paycheck. If you have made a commitment to pay for a vehicle and to insure it, you need to meet those obligations before you spend on things you want. Setting up an emergency fund and a savings account will help you manage your money, and a budget will guide you in your spending so you can meet your obligations as well as save for those things you want.

Note to Parents: We need to teach our children how to handle their money. If we supply them with spending money and the monetary gifts they receive for birthdays, etc., they need to use this money wisely. Teach them while they are young so they will be wise with their spending when they have their own job. Make sure you are setting a good example for your children in your own spending.

Learn how to spend your money wisely while you are still young.

- Ask your parents to help you set up a savings account with a portion of whatever money you receive.
- Beware of reckless spending. Learn to save for the things you want while you are still young.
- If you have a job, meeting your needs should be the priority each time you receive a paycheck.

- If you have made a commitment to pay for a vehicle and to insure it, you need to meet those obligations before you spend on things you want.
- Setting up an emergency fund will help you manage your money.
- A budget will guide you in your spending so you can meet your obligations as well as save for those things you want.

#11:

LOVE AND RELATIONSHIPS

You need to understand the meaning of love and how to control your emotions. Love is one of the best things in life. You need love in everything you do in life. Love can be heavy or strong and light or weak. You need to know how to use it in balance. Parents have a special love for our families. We want to see our kids have a better and happier life than we did.

Children, please, do not think that when we are a little hard on you it is because we don't love you. We are doing that because we do love you and we want what is best for you.

Learning to develop quality relationships as you become teenagers and young adults is very important. A good quality man or woman will have beauty inside. It will show the way they act on the outside. These are the type of people you want to fall in love with and spend your adult life with.

Children, this area of your life is very slippery. You need to be careful where you're walking. It's so easy to fall and most of the time it isn't easy to get back at your feet. You need to think hard before you make your decision to give your love to another person of the opposite gender.

When you are eighteen and up, you need to understand what dating can mean to your future. You don't need a boyfriend or girlfriend because of sex. You need to prepare for meeting your future spouse. You need to date for some years to get to know them and determine if that person can be your best choice for a husband or wife. You need to take sex out of it. Because, sex can be addicted. Once you start it, there is a 95 percent chance you will not stop it. Sometimes that can cause your relationship to fall apart a week or two later.

First step: when you graduate from high School. You are going to the prom celebration to have a good time. Please, do not forget you are not going to a wedding. You are doing to celebrate your hard work that you did. You can choose any one that you want, like one of your family or one of your best friends. You can enjoy yourself to the fullest and you need to go home not in a hotel. Do not forget that wasn't a wedding.

Second steps: now you are ready for your college degree. You need to do the same thing as you did as high school. It just takes a little hard work. Then you will earn your college degree.

Third steps: now you are ready for your wonderful husband and wife you have been dating. You guys get married and have children. If you want to be a good mother and father. Do not use me as an example. You need to use yourself as an example.

Please don't make the same mistake like I did and not realize what reckless dating can mean to your future relationships. The evil part is what you give away you never get back to give to the person who will appreciate it and be special in your life. You need to stop thinking that life is a joke. The longer you live, the more you learn.

I'm Haitian and my girlfriend is from St. Lucia. I never disrespect her in any kind of way. I love and respect my family. Many people are choosing relationships by religion or race. They have many relationships which don't last long because of the choices they make. That unhealthy relationship will not take you to the place you really want to spend for the rest of your life. Please, don't let your mind make you see things don't exist. Choose to date wisely because it will affect your future.

Children, choose wisely when you begin dating.

- You need to understand what dating can mean to your future.
- Take sex out of it.
- You need to date for some years to get to know and determine if that person can be your best choice for a husband or wife.
- Please, don't let your heart make you see things don't exist in your relationship. If you are making excuses for their behavior, you need to think twice about continuing that relationship.

#12:

FEAR IS YOUR WORST ENEMY

When you go to school, always keep in mind that some people are going to like you and some will not. You need to be prepared for that. You need to try your best to be friends with smart students who choose to do things right and avoid the bully.

Listen to my story. When I was a kid, I wasn't lazy in school. I became friends with smart students who were serious about learning. I liked school and I wanted to be an "A" student, but it was not easy for me. Anything I had difficulty with, I asked my friends to show me how to do it. We used to work together and share everything that we knew.

If you take this as an example and you stay away from bullies, you will enjoy school just like I did. Even though things are hard, never make up your mind it is too hard.

Your fears are your worst enemies. Always make yourself think you can achieve whatever you set your mind to and you will see how easy you will get it done. Sometimes, you need to learn how to challenge yourself so you can see how far you can get. Anything that you do in life can make it interesting and fun if you choose to do things the right way. This is what life is all about.

I give this information to you to pass on from generation to generation. The worst thing in your life is to make yourself look stupid. You need to see that when you choose wisely, work hard, and respect others, you will be able to walk together with others who will help you move forward in life.

I am giving you this information to help you to grow up like a productive human being. It is your choice. It will be your responsibility to get your job done right, but you need to know every choice has a consequence, good or bad. If it comes out good, you can keep the trophy, but if it comes out bad you can only blame yourself.

Your fears are your worst enemies. To conquer them:

- Always think you can achieve whatever you set your mind to and you will see how easy you will get it done.
- Sometimes, you need to learn how to challenge yourself so you can see how far you can get.

- Anything that you do in life can make it interesting and fun if you choose to do things the right way. This is what life is all about.
- Remember, every choice has a consequence, good or bad. If it comes out good, you can keep the trophy, but if it comes out bad you can only blame yourself. The choice is yours!

In the Bible, 2 Timothy 1:7 says, "For God gave us a spirit not of fear but of power and love and self-control" (ESV).

#13:

Learn from our Mistakes

L ife is something we need to seek to understand. By the time you are thirteen, you know what is right and what is wrong. Your parents have been working hard to take care of you and want you to learn from what they have done, good and bad. They want you to learn not to make the same mistakes they did and not have to let what happened to them happen to you.

You need to learn from your parents' mistakes. You need to ask questions and we will make sure that we give you the right answer. This is the way life works. None of us shouldn't keep making the same mistakes our parents made. Your future life is your "land" which is your life. You have a choice of seeds to plant in your "land." You need to select seeds to plant that produce the "fruit" you want to grow in it. If you want healthy fruit growing in it, you have to take care of it properly. If you do not take care of this earth and your life, you will get an unhealthy crop. This is your choice. I hope that you open your eyes before it's too late.

You make excuses when you come home with your report card with a big fat "F" in it and get angry with us when we reprimand you for it. We know you can do better and that you must do the work required to improve your grades because they reflect what you are or are not learning. As parents, we can't really tell you how to live your life, but we can give you some examples from real life to make you think of doing the right things.

For example, you can wear any type of clothes you want, but if you want to do a good job for yourself, you need to know when to wear them and when to dress more professionally. You are unique and special in your own way and you can make your own choices, but there are times you will need to do things and make choices professionally. If you choose to do things right, later you will not have to worry about a thing that you did in the past coming back to haunt you.

God tells us clearly; we will reap from the kinds of seeds we sow into our lives and even in others. Read Galatians 6:7-10 in the Bible.

Learn from our Mistakes

- You need to try your best to do things right because one silly mistake can haunt you for the rest of your life.
- When you are young, you want to try every crazy thing in life, but you never think about how it will haunt you after.
- Everything you do will walk with you in the future and others will use it against you.

If you choose to do things right, later you will not have to worry about a thing that you did in the past coming back to haunt you.

#14:

Learn to Work Together

You need to take care of your own business before you waste your time worrying about other people's business. You are wasting your time looking at others and what they have and they do. You don't even know how far away you are from where you could be if you focused on what you should be doing right now. Why do you let what others are doing drag you in an unhealthy direction?

Some people are bullies and they will never want to see you move forward. Those people had great opportunities at one time, but now they waste time bullying and preying on others. They missed the plan that was right for them worrying about what others were doing. You need to stop and realize what you are doing and where you are going is in the wrong direction. If not, you will end up just like those others. You really need to think very hard about this and pick something great that you want to do with your life. Then pursue that instead of mimicking others.

I feel it is my responsibility to teach you what is right and wrong. I'm the coach and you are the players. I know you will do things that I didn't teach you. It will be alright, but try your best to do it right. Most of the things you will learn on your own. I just want to help you build a stronger base which will hold the building you really want to build in your life. You need to try your best to learn as much as you can. You need to get ready for this crazy world. Day-by-day the world is getting crazier. You are the one who will control the planet. I just want to see you get it going in a better direction. I know you can do it. Life is so sweet and simple.

One way to begin to do this is to start working together with others who want to see a productive change right now. You are brothers and sisters. This planet is going to belong to your generation very soon. If you don't take care of it, no one will. You need to change the direction this world is heading.

These are the magic words that will help you remember how to begin to change the direction for your good and the good of your generation:

Picture how a hand works together to accomplish a task

Thumb - Support each other.
Index Finger - Appreciate each other.

Middle Finger - Respect each other.
Ring Finger - Love each other.
Pinky Finger – Pull Them all together.

If you use these five magic words, you will see how different your planet will be compared to my planet. You have five fingers and you need all of them to work properly. You need to try your best to use them together and never leave anyone of them behind.

I remember a cartoon called Tom and Jerry. These two could never stop fighting with each other. Do not behave like Tom and Jerry. You need to stop fighting and arguing all the time with your siblings. Do you know why your little brother and sister don't respect you? You are doing it wrong. You are not disciplining him or her. You are just bothering them and bullying them. As a big brother and sister, you need to learn how to listen to them and learn what they like or not. You need to try to understand them and talk to them with respect. Make them feel like you love them and you will be there for them.

I was a big brother. I was there for them like a father. If you don't want to stop it or change the way you are acting toward your little brother and sister, you will never earn their respect. You need to focus and start to learn to be a better older sister or brother toward your younger siblings. This will help you as you enter the workforce and become a parent yourself.

Time to Learn to Work Together to Bring Change:

- First, you need to learn to be a better older sister or brother. This will help you as you enter the workforce and become a parent yourself.
- Next, you need to stop mimicking others. This is the wrong path.
- You really need to think very hard and pick something great that you want to do with your life.
- Then pursue that instead of mimicking others.

Picture how the fingers and thumb on your hand work together to accomplish a task:

Thumb - Support each other.
Index Finger - Appreciate each other.
Middle Finger - Respect each other.
Ring Finger - Love each other.
Pinky Finger – Pull Them all together.

You have five fingers and you need all of them to work properly. You need to work with others like your hand to bring about change and make the world a better place for you, your family, and future generations as well.

#15:

Secrets

What is the meaning of a secret? A secret means it is not something you should just share with everyone. No matter how old or young you are, you need to know there are things you should talk about to others and things you shouldn't talk about with them. You need to try to understand the people who are around you. You need to trust everyone within a limit. Sometimes, you think you know them, but be careful. As humans, we seem to want to know the business of everyone.

Listen to yourself talking. You should never tell anyone another person's secrets. When someone tells you something, you must keep it secret. It is not yours to share. You are not a messenger. If he or she wants to talk about their business with someone else, it is their choice. Please, do not be a gossip or share what someone has told you about themselves or someone else.

Remember, everyone makes mistakes. We need to be careful about talking about them with others. You also need to learn the difference between making a mistake and doing something foolish. A mistake is something you do, but you didn't know that you shouldn't do it. A mistake is something you think you were going to get done right, but it ends up wrong. You can avoid many mistakes by double-checking before you do something that might then be a mistake. That doesn't mean that you won't make mistakes, but it will happen less often. I'm not perfect and I don't think anyone is, but I try my best to say I'm sorry when I have done something I find out has been a mistake.

Being dumb means that you are ignorant, or you are not too smart, or you are smart in a special way. Being foolish, however, is when you know for sure things you are doing are not right, but you do it anyway. That is being foolish. Please, don't be that person. I know for sure none of us are perfect. This is the reason I'm trying to prepare you for the future.

How do we avoid making mistakes and acting foolishly?

- Do not be a gossip or share what someone has told you about themselves or someone else.

- Remember, everyone makes mistakes. We need to be careful about talking about them with others.
- You also need to learn the difference between making a mistake and doing something foolish.
- A mistake is something you do, but you didn't know that you shouldn't do it. Apologize right away when this happens.
- Being foolish, however, is when you know for sure things you are doing are not right, but you do it anyway. Do not be foolish!

#16:

Respect Yourself and Others

Respect is something that you need to own for yourself. No one will respect you unless you respect yourself. Let me give you the details of respect. First of all, you can be rich or poor, that doesn't have anything to do with respect. When you are a respectful person and you do things the right way, you earn and give respect. When you know that you are wrong, you need to always apologize. You need to tell the truth and stop lying to others or yourself. When you borrow from others, you need to give it back in a timely manner. Do not take advantage of others. Try to depend on yourself. Never take anything that doesn't belong to you. Do not hang out with people who don't respect themselves. Try to be professional in every case.

Your job is something you want to keep and comes with a big responsibility. You need to know why you are there. You are working because this is the right thing to do. You need to take care of yourself and your loved ones. You need to take your work and responsibility seriously. That is not a place you go or do whatever you want. You need to respect their rules. You need to make sure you are on time and do the job you are assigned to the very best of your ability. You just need to do things the right way. If you don't want to work there anymore, you need to keep doing your job the right way until you find another job. Never push anyone under the bus.

Don't forget you are representing the company to its customers. You need to make sure the company's reputation is respected. It doesn't matter if you like the company or not. If you like the company and you want to stay working there for a long time, you need to learn how to work your way to the top, but not at the expense of your fellow workers. I worked as a manager for more than fifteen years for the hotel laundry companies. I started from the lowest paying position and I worked my way up to the plant manager position. You know you need to work hard to achieve your goals. There were people who wanted to see me fail, but I didn't because I knew what I was there for and I diligently did my job.

Do not let anyone think they know you better than you know yourself and always try your best to do things right.

Respect Yourself and Others

I truly believe that you will have a happy life, but you are the one who will make it happen. No one will do it for you.

Respect Requires Respect
This is a very important Life Lesson.

- When you are a respectful person and you do things the right way, you earn and give respect.
- When you know that you are wrong, you need to always apologize.
- You need to be truthful and stop lying to others.
- When you borrow from others, you need to give it back in a timely manner.
- Do not take advantage of others. Try to depend on yourself.
- Never take anything that doesn't belong to you.
- Do not hang out with people who don't respect themselves.
- You need to take your work and responsibility seriously and respect their rules. You need to make sure you are on time and do the job you are assigned to the very best of your ability.
- You just need to do things the right way and make sure the company's reputation is respected.

#17:

ALL LIVES MATTER

You need to always remember that all lives matter. Killing another living thing is not a sport. You must never kill someone or something unless your life or a loved one's life is in danger. Some people kill animals for sport. I know the meaning of the food chain, but we can kill only what we need to survive. Life is not a joke and every life is important. Please, learn the meaning of all lives matter. The world is yours. Treat it with respect and care.

If you really have faith in the Lord and you follow His rules, there isn't anything you won't be able to do. Moses and the other biblical leaders followed God's rules and were able to fulfill God's purpose in their lives. They were able to help change the world for their future generations.

You need to respect yourself and others. You need to stop fighting with your brother and sister. Stop killing each other, stop bullying each other, stop lying to each other, stop telling lies about others to stop them moving forward, and stop holding each other back so you can get ahead. Working together is the best way to get the job done. You need to have each other's back and watch for each other's mistakes. You need to start having a positive attitude through faith in God because our Lord has promised us He will not leave us alone. He always will be here with us as long we have faith in Him. I'm telling you the truth and the realities of life.

I'm not going to tell you to not have fun like going to the beach, parties, churches, etc. This is what life is for and you need to enjoy it until the end, but you need to know what fun is about. Pay attention! Do not have fun at the expense of others. Let us all learn to do things right so we can receive the blessing from the Lord.

Students used to pray in school, but now everything has changed. We are going in the wrong direction. We are hurting ourselves and we don't even realize it. Be all that God has called us to be and begin to do and stand up for what is right in every area of your life. You will see positive change and make the world a better place for your generation and the generations to come.

Conclusion

Promises from God

Eleanor Roosevelt once said, "No one can make you feel inferior without your consent." Whenever insecurities rear their ugly head, the Bible encourages us to replace their lies with truth. To do that we need to read the Bible daily and study it so we know the promises God has given us and the truth He wants us to live by. Here are some to get you started.

In 2 Corinthians 1:20, the Bible tells us, "For all the promises of God in Him are Yes, and in Him Amen, to the glory of God through us." The promises of God are rock solid. If God said something, it would come to pass. When you trust in the Lord with all your heart and believe Him at His Word, you can and will receive His promises. God isn't like man, His promises are guaranteed.

One very important promise you can only receive by doing things God's way is found in Exodus 20:12, "Honor your father and your mother, that your days may be long upon the land which the LORD your God is giving you" (NKJV).

The Bible proclaims in Psalm 27:10 that even if your father and mother forsake you, the Lord will hold you close. He is the eternal lover of your soul and He will never abandon you. He has even promised to supply your needs if you do things His way.

In Matthew 6:33, Jesus said, "But seek first the kingdom of God and his righteousness, and all these things shall be added to you" (NKJV). His way means you cannot place other things before the Lord. You need to put Him first in all things. That is the right way and the right order to receive blessings from God in your life.

God also wants you to be equipped to handle the trials and storms of life that will surely come your way. Jesus never promised you no troubles would come your way while you are living here on earth, but He has made available to you what you need to not only survive but have a victorious and prosperous life. Jesus said in John 16:33, "I have told you these things, so that in me you may have peace. In this world you will have trouble. But take heart! I have overcome the world" (NIV).

Philippians 4:13 tells you to declare, "I can do all things through Christ who strengthens me" (NKJV). If you rely only on your own strength, you will fall short. If you rely on God, He will give you His strength and power to overcome in this world. His promise to you is you can do all things through Him, not without Him.

God has also said you do not have to live in fear. 2 Timothy 1:7 says, "For God gave us a spirit not of fear but of power and love and self-control" (ESV). You need self-control to continually do things the right way. Whatever He tells you to do, He will give you what you need to accomplish it if you just seek His help. The only way to do that is to spend time with Him every day, reading the Bible and talking with Him about what you are facing each day.

One of the greatest promises from God is found in Jeremiah 29:11, "'For I know the plans I have for you,' says the Lord, 'plans to prosper you and not to harm you, plans to give you hope and a future'" (NIV). God's plan for your life includes hope and a prosperous future, one in which you thrive.

In fact, Psalm 103:2-5 lists the many ways God wants to bless you. "Praise the Lord, O my soul, and forget not all his benefits - who forgives all your sins and heals all your diseases, who redeems your life from the pit and crowns you with love and compassion, who satisfies your desires with good things so that your youth is renewed like the eagle's" (NIV).

As I have said many times throughout this book, you need to work together with others to become all that God has said you are able to accomplish His plans for you. Jesus explains the power of working together when He states, "For where two or three gather in my name, there am I with them" (Matthew 18:20 NIV). Coming together allows God to reveal Himself to you and then you can reveal God's amazing promises to others.

CPSIA information can be obtained
at www.ICGtesting.com
Printed in the USA
BVHW032343280321
603512BV00023B/298